in the voice of trees

AN ANTHOLOGY OF TREE LORE

Edited by Jan Fortune & Adam Craig

GW00503234

Cinnamon Press
:: small miracles from distinctive voices ::

Published by Cinnamon Press, Meirion House, Glan yr afon,
Tanygrisiau. Blaenau Ffestiniog,Gwynedd, LL41 3SU

www.cinnamonpress.com

The right of the authors to be identified as the authors of this
work has been asserted by them in accordance with the
Copyright, Designs and Patent Act, 1988. © 2020 the authors.

ISBN 978-1-78864-090-9

British Library Cataloguing in Publication Data. A CIP record for
this book can be obtained from the British Library.

Designed and typeset by Cinnamon Press.
Cover illustration: GDJ / Pixabay.

Cinnamon Press is represented in the UK by Inpress Ltd
www.inpressbooks.co.uk and in Wales by the Books Council of
Wales www.cllc.org.uk

Contents

Jude O Mahony

Hawthorn

Sea pinks stem from salted rock.
Fetch of wind catches white sun's light.
Red   orange   Yellow
swell to Atlantic blue.
Scattering white capped clusters of
mother-dye.

Joan McGavin

Willow

I look through my window at the moon.
It looks back, wipes me clean of sleep.

I've heard it smells of gunpowder.
There's no way to check.

I see how craggy its face has become.
How small my bump of a nose must seem

by comparison. And how silently
the moon displays my neighbour's willow

as fireworks'
fallout

Gail Ashton

When

they felled the oak
down the lane

birds stopped singing
and ours shed her last

winter leaves in shock.
At night her breathing

slowed. I heard her
heartwood knock knock

against the glass
of stars. And even now

she wears the call
of owls not knowing

how to be still
ever fill the space…

Birch

Wood reads the air, finds it wanting.
Speaks moss and birch, is raining deer.
Lives between words of hollow light,

fallen late to shape a stream. Knows
those things that do not linger.
Carries a place we thought was winter.

indoors for much of the winter

emptying the dregs
of evening into a bowl

moon at a window wanting
to come in and you are

a vision with your life
of torn petticoats

hands a skeleton of ash
trees pointing up light

Janet Olearski

Lost

Under this tree of lost things,
a child's pencil, a key. A glove,
pointing to the road we cannot see.
A broken watch, an exposed cable,
cream to remove wrinkled plans.
An embedded horseshoe, a rope,
notes still unread, an aspirin.
A beer bottle, empty of courage.
String, length as yet unknown.
Will no one reclaim what is lost?

David Olsen

Silver Birches

1.
Yellow leaves
engrave evanescent names
into early snow.

2.
A century after the French fled
the breath of General Winter,
sleigh runners glissando through fresh crust.

Distant bells toll;
troika bells jingle
through ringing air.

Beneath crystal stars, a young woman
in fur rugs breathes blades,
dreams of white nights in June.

3.
Old woman's funeral:
Slavonic chants aspire
beyond bare birches.

Jean Hall

The Relict Tree

It grows where no trees grow,
on the edge of a gully,

safe from grazing sheep
until winter builds ice bridges

A site of special interest,
reminder of an ancient woodland past:

a layer of bark, stiff with sheen,
traces of knots, side-branch scars,

a time of willow, aspen, birch,
wild roses and honeysuckle,

dense coppices where blackbirds
nested and once sang.

The hazel's deep-veined branches
and its shrub companions:

spindly, sparsely-berried rowan,
thorny strands of dog-rose

resist 100-miles-an-hour winds creaming
cliffs, exposing glaciated slopes, travelling

like us, down every road
from Muckle Flugga to Sunburgh.

We walked those landscapes,
found meaning in a cargo of centuries,

laughed with loons, heard storytellers
of doom, seen crofts and cairns,

brochs in fog, sea-stacks, lighthouses,
rich oceans of flock and fin,

caught crab and mackerel,
dined on tasty seaweed lamb,

heard a choir of kittiwakes, sang with seals,
sighted gannets, guillemots and puffins,

shared bus shelters with sheep,
muzzled by midges at dusk.

On beaches we trawled for fossils,
driftwood shapes and stones to take home.

Memories thrive, like the relict tree
still growing, even though you have left.

Vivienne Tregenza

Elder

> *And in the tree there sat a sweet-looking old woman in a very strange dress...*
>> 'Hyldemoer' by Hans Christian Anderson

Who will I be when you've stripped me bare,
when you've shaken

the lacework from my pithy stems
to make your potions?

Will the white mist come kiss me again?
Will the wind still whisper my name?

What will you make of me with your stolen twigs?
Wish-sticks! May they turn against you...

May your flutes summon only
ghosts from the graveyards,

hear them sigh
like restless trees in winter.

Should you uproot me, try to craft
my twisted limbs into a cot, I'll turn

and take what's mine.

Allotment

So we rejected their plan
to put us on the plot adjacent

to the bare brown earth, sprayed
with systemic God-knows-what.

We sensed our child's need
to make mud pies and taste the soil,

chose the patch beneath the hedge;
wild flowers jostling for space,

an apple tree flushed and heavy
with fruit, a blackberry bush

entangled in the raspberry canes.
We came to love the weeds,

tenaciously ignored pleas
to *Keep things tidy*.

Art Ó Súilleabháin

Irish Oak

Years seasoning, thin staves,
hard as iron, pliable for a moment,
from the long black melting pot.

Infuse strength with beads of bog water,
fill with unforgiving power poured into rigid timber,
ability to bend for a moment, blackened in a cast-iron pipe.
It sets again to hold the shape of boat, ribs dried against larch.

Oars

Their hand-shaped bos a pleasure in the feel of outer curve
sitting there, between the fishing priests, truth only spoken
when required, but there, reliable and countable in idleness.

Like truths in my own life, that would row to any destination
chosen by those seeking to pull or back rowing into bays
of content or discontent, row-locks protesting noisily.

Sue Moules

Ivy

Holds the fence together,
dark green leaves
tendrils tights over rotten wood
spreading
along and around,
roots deep into soil.
I clip its wisps
for my Christmas wreath.

Donna Kirstein

Visits with trees

Birch

The birch waits quietly in the field
and you are drawn towards
her pale white skin, luminous
in the gloaming. Each moment is a gift.
Her leaves shimmer in the fading light
as day turns night and seasons burn
sunlight sparks off leaves - crisp
like electricity underfoot.
But the wind whispers winter.

Rowan

Late night walks in the depth of autumn
When Bridget wraps her talisman
around your neck,
her fingers soft, brushing
the hair from your cheek,
quickening your pulse,
telling tales of rowan's energy
and with each touch you feel
your soul unfold.

Alder

The catalyst was an alder tree,
strong and bold she thrived and in thriving
spread her arms and shed her cares,
tossing seeds like thoughts to the wind
to catch and spread like lichen
slowly rooting down,
solidly seeking water, knowing
the time will come, the sprouting
is inevitable.

Willow

Sitting under the willow while rain
whittles its way down the branches
to the waters edge, carving rivulets into the earth
as it prepares to join the community
of water. Beyond the clouds the moon
begins to rise alone, and in another
place a woman howls her grief
into the night, casting
her memories adrift into a sea of stars.

Ash

Ash trees leaves are pinnately compound
each matched in a perfect pair,
but it's winter and her budding
leaves are soft dark velvet,
her canopy will only form in spring.
But for now you can start to see
how she moves, her branches shield
the life within. Her leaves will turn,
bending, will grow towards
the warm truth of sunlight.

Hawthorn

Walking through woodland,
lining the hedgerows you come across
a bent backed hawthorn,
her skin bark rough and knotted,
yet under her dense prickles she shelters
a swarm of survivors.
When spring comes
the May-tree blooms, unfurling
her scent into the wind.

Oak

The oak stands tall, rooted deep,
confident of her place and strength
of will, a doorway into the inner
world. Look to her when you need
support. In spring, you will come to realise
that when her love flowers,
male, female, it matters not.
The fruit will follow, small
bitter acorns will mature and fall.

Holly

The holly bush is popular
amongst the birds. She spreads
her branches and seeds her drupes,
the scarification process proceeds,
as stones are swallowed and scattered,
each one a kernel of tightly wound
sharp leaves, waiting to explore
their potential when the white wood
of the shrub sprouts.

Hazel

When the yellow catkins hang
against the winter trees
you can't miss hazel. Her small red
flowers tassel the branches, throwing
pollen against the air, reminding you
of another hazel, whose face
was covered with soft-bud like freckles
and who moved without caution
through the summer sun.

Apple

After the slow heat of summer,
when autumn finally comes,
with her abundance of apples,
falling to the floor, you will
find yourself, under the full
moon, the sweet tang
of a forbidden fruit
on your tongue
juice lingering on your lips.

Ivy

When journeying through this otherworld,
and an ivy thicket evolves, take heed
and pause to search for aspects
of yourself. In the fall
when flowers bloom,
feeding and fruiting into the winter,
while host trees provide support
her roots will dig deep
to find the nutrients needed.

Elder

As seasons turn the elder follows
the cycle and you will come across
her standing in a field, a crone
guarding the under-inner world,
her branches outstretched,
to welcome you, casting a spell of
fruit and flowers across the year.
When broken off, each hollow fire
branch will grab and root and grow again.

Tim Kiely

Julian's Vision of the Hazelnut

So little, this   impossible.
Enough to stagger everything:

this ball of ghostly understanding
given wholly into your

untutored palm;
   palpitating;

skin alive with nebulae;
nameless; known; altogether

fluttering its heavenly
weight.

So little it was enough to ask,
"What may this be?"

and then be answered
generally,

"It is all that is made."

Patricia Helen Wooldridge

Hazel Prelude

The time of the singing of birds is come

Song of Solomon 2:12

Christmas leavings
red on graves

river of clouds surging

yellow lichen
absorbing stone

puddles shimmering

catkins loosening
sixty-five years

before I see

tiny red stars on stalks
that were always there

Measuring the Oak
(at Steep Church)

No-one here except the dead
two red kites floating

the trough of air
held by the hill —

a February too warm
daffodils too soon

both of us hugging
the largest oak —

two thousand felled
for one ship —

our arms not meeting —
Elizabethan

Alder Carr

Walk the purple haze
of long-mapped carr

pass the orange wounds
stacked in clearings

scan high among cones
for siskins

weaving the river
flexing into March

Birch Standings

For Clare, one strip of bark
    yields ten sheets of paper

I reach to impressions
    painted on my eye

with their shocks of hair
    stretched in the wind

At the Edge of the Wind
(after Hockney's Hawthorn Blossom)

With every green
remarked in silk

wooded boundaries
shivering

hover by
stippled light

cow parsley
under armfuls

of hawthorn
brimming-over-cream

Chorus for the Ash

All around us, ash trees are quietly dying

How long for the black velvet buds
rising in our garden

while woods are skeletal
canopies spare

or the jackdaws' garrulous
ash tree hub

forays into dusk?

Spread-finger leaves
for sky to breathe

why we chose this house —
not for the rending scars

when a branch swings down
brackets shoulder into view —

how long?

O willow ...

sway across the river
like a bough at sea

where mind and water
overflow

watching willow

Elder Picking

Around the time
elderberries
drop into black

my pen
on a wet afternoon
dips into ink

Pausing by the Rowan

Slow burn
melds into rowan

equinox time
from the mountain

turns the corner
into

hanging fists
of vermillion

Apple Thinking

Each drop of rain
a speck of dust
on a sea wind

pink flush
sucked
to its core

a cloak of skin
easing
summer

squat
       heavy
              yellow belly

falls in the hand
at shore

Ode to the Ivy

Thrum of bees
deep in November

spiralling den
of the woods

star bursts
loop-along-hedge

ripen slow
clinging on

enough for redwings
to gorge

Holly Red

Scarlet beads in lowering sun
    so cold

survives ice age, dinosaurs,
    any hacking down

scarlet beads on white winter
    so cold

not one berry left in December

Stan Galloway

Entering the Dnipro at Dawn

A birch stations itself
                on the south bit of the island
white bark
        a sentry's staff holding back the sea
brandishing crinkled leaves
        glinting drachmas of a bygone trader
to rebuff all the eons
           blunders
           breaches passed and
   welcome all that blossom ahead.

Shoreline North of Zaporizhia

Moonlight sieved through willow on the river
        lapping shore sensuously, soft, light, tree-lensed
sotto voce of hosannas year round in bandura strings
inscribed in pysanka swirls and infants' tongues
        marketplace boxes, handcrafts, satiny veneers
shimmy of soles woven in tanned leather, soothing
dulling the (s)weep of unremembered ancestry.

In the Carpathian Foothills

One varicoloured oak
on the doorstep of oaks   delimits
       resilience
crowned over alder and ivy
beside a slender
          upland
            trail
leading from carp pond and ditches
dreams centuries-old
hope sodden with silence
damp limbs tentacular and unyielding
its glinting leaves hobbled words of prophecy

Hazel

Who considers your gloves and clogs
in the dusk-dance of the Dnister lowland
        inconspicuous
decades coppiced and conscious
ambisexual catkins pink
                yellow
ribbed, elliptic leaves episodic
smooth bark
tan-cream-grey
creases, puckers really,
security for moths in Autumn
witness to caliginous skies
scratching at western wind
nut-thoughts coloured season-by-season
unconcerned with chaotic human landscapes?

Nigel Hutchinson

(birch)

heather-coloured carpet
stretches to french windows
edge of heathland
birch trees' silvery bark
marks a path through
late afternoon's broken sun
away from today's traffic
of human voices
to that rhythm
of inbreath-outbreath-inbreath
a cycle of beginnings
and endings
oxygen carbon oxygen carbon
oxygen-carbon-oxygen-carbon
oxygencarbonoxygencarbon

Vincent Steed

Union

Our lives weave different avenues
since that tree-lined viscous morning.
Intermittent shafts of light
connect like rosary beads
prayers of what might have been
stimulate miracles in the undergrowth.
Our car stalls on the gravel path,
the doe magnificent momentarily.
With fawn in tow - all hip and elbow
and for that unsullied second
child and mother union is sacred.

Lynn Valentine

Night's Breath

Bright moon and willow nod,
pale sisters under ink sky
light the way for dawn.

Hazel

Each leaf glazed in gold,
a molten whisky morning
warms passing footsteps.

Emily Vanderploeg

The Fool
(alder: *looking to the future*)

This is how you see yourself.

Wise enough to leap
from the cliff, but
fool enough to guess at
where you're going

Pack your satchel
and bring along your familiars.

Do not be afraid to look
straight at the sun.

Three of Wands
(willow: *the moon, its rhythms and tides*)

Your beloved bay recedes.
It's time to go, the ships are coming in.

But oh, still you cling
to the echo of his tenor, your soul father,
all *hiraeth*, all ache.

Your three loves,
that grew as if by magic, now
washed away with the winter run-off
and the rubbish that rides
the tides.

Queens, Minor Arcana
(hawthorn: *transformation; enchantment and change*)

This is you right now.

A queen of the senses;
shades of sweet green, yarrow,
stars in a sunlit sky.

When all of a sudden
the trees have leafed —
a clean white feather at your feet
and you cannot see
the sea.

The Tower
(oak: *strength, courage and resilience*)

This is what you fear
and what you hope for:

To jump
from the burning tower

or, to roll
over the falls in a barrel.

Either way, something changes.

Every bone is broken,
but washed clean, too.

Zoe Broom

Homcoming

Wild waves wail after sunset
splashing sails on ships struggling home.
A beckoning becomes beyond us now.
Beyond broken horizon, all is black.

Laura Wainwright

Rowan

Summer closing down. Rusting roofs failing, falling in, leaf
by curled leaf.

A turn ahead in the path and the month, winding, knurled
and ivied, down.

On the Mountain Ash carnelian beads bunch, daub the sky,
charm its sheer Miró blue.

Fruit is air and armour

ceci est la coleur

My eyes feast like October birds

*This poem draws inspiration from Juan Miro's 1925 painting
'Photo — Ceci est la coleur de mes réves'*

Ness Owen

Cerddinen

That first winter
I thought I'd lost
you, the toughest
of survivors, they
said, so I tended
your bareness
willed for the
poem inside you
to bud, watched
for pinnate fingers
waited for the berries
I would sew in hem-
lines, to guard all
that I love.